Assert yourself

How to find your voice and
make your mark

BLOOMSBURY

A BLOOMSBURY REFERENCE BOOK
Created from the Bloomsbury Business Database
www.ultimatebusinessresource.com

© Bloomsbury Publishing Plc 2004

First published in 2004 by
Bloomsbury Publishing Plc
38 Soho Square
London W1D 3HB

British Library Cataloguing in Publication Data
A CIP record for this book is available from the British Library.

ISBN 0–7475–7205–4

Design by Fiona Pike, Pike Design, Winchester
Typeset by RefineCatch Limited, Bungay, Suffolk
Printed by Clausen & Bosse, Leck, Germany

All papers used by Bloomsbury Publishing are natural, recyclable
products made from wood grown in well-managed forests. The
manufacturing processes conform to the environmental regulations
of the country of origin.

Contents

How assertive are you?

Answer the questions and work out where you are on the assertiveness scale, then read the guidance points for ideas on how to get the most positive response from those around you.

How often do you feel 'put upon' at work?
a) Regularly, but it is what I expect.
b) I generally feel in control of my workload.
c) Colleagues have finally realised that I am not to be imposed upon.

How do you feel when someone seeks your opinion?
a) Very grateful as it happens so rarely.
b) I feel happy that they value my judgments.
c) Colleagues usually know my opinions already—if they have to ask they weren't listening!

It's your annual review and you feel you deserve a decent pay rise. Which is closest to your approach?
a) I wait for them to mention it. They know their budgets.
b) I explain how I've progressed, and why I deserve a rise.
c) I demand a pay rise—or else!

You're having a discussion with someone who isn't giving you a chance to respond. What do you do?

a) Wait and listen. They may have something valuable to say.
b) Make eye contact and let my body language show I'm about to speak, before starting to make my point.
c) Talk louder than them—they'll soon stop and listen!

If a colleague asks you to do something which isn't in your job remit, what do you do?
a) Try to fit it in—it's important to be as helpful as possible.
b) It may provide a useful learning experience, so try to fit it in, but make sure they know I'm doing them a favour.
c) Refuse—it's their job and their responsibility.

How do you feel about your managers?
a) I worry that they don't think much of me.
b) I respect their experience. We're all on the same team.
c) I don't think much of them, so try to avoid them so I can get on with my job.

A colleague stops by to chat but stays too long, preventing you from getting on with your work. What do you do?
a) Let them stay, and resign myself to staying late to finish.
b) Explain that I have a deadline to meet and suggest they return another time.
c) Tell them to stop bothering me—can't they see I'm busy?

You suspect a colleague dislikes you, but aren't sure why. How do you deal with this?
a) Pretend I'm unaware of their attitude and try my best to avoid them.
b) Talk to them to find out the reason for their aversion.
c) Be confrontational in my dealings with them so that next time they will think twice about being haughty.

a = **1, b** = **2, and c** = **3.** Now add up your scores.

Chapter **1** is useful to everyone as it suggests different ways of projecting a more positive image, including paying attention to body language and reacting differently to different character types.

- **8–13:** You're at the passive end of the assertiveness scale, and if you're not careful you'll end up being taken for granted which will make you very unhappy. Assertiveness is not simply about talking more and louder; read chapter **2** to discover new ways of developing presence—let people know you are there! Learn how to control others' perceptions of you by reading chapter **5**. Bullying is never acceptable. If you think you're being treated unfairly or being bullied, chapter **6** offers advice on dealing with your situation.
- **14–18:** You have a balanced, assertive approach to your work and colleagues, which would be good to build upon. Develop your non-verbal communication and leadership skills (chapters **5** and **7**) in order to hone your abilities and achieve your full potential.
- **19–24:** You're in danger of being aggressive and making enemies. Perhaps your behaviour stems from a lack of confidence in your abilities, and you're overcompensating for this. Chapters **3** and **7** offer ideas for building confidence. Remember to communicate effectively by listening actively and mirroring your colleagues' body language (chapters **2** and **4**). You're all working for the same side, so you don't feel the need to compete for supremacy!

Communicating assertively at work

Do you find that people get the better of you at work, that you're not given the respect you deserve, or that you're always the one who draws the short straw and ends up doing things that you would rather not do? Does this end up making you resentful or unhappy because you feel helpless and unable to confront the situation?

Assertiveness is an approach to communication that honours your choices as well as those of the person you are communicating with. It's not about being aggressive and steamrollering your colleagues into submission. Rather, it's about seeking and exchanging opinions, developing a full understanding of the issues, and negotiating a win-win situation.

Ask yourself these questions to determine your level of assertiveness:

■ Do you feel 'put upon' or ignored in your exchanges with colleagues?
■ Are you unable to speak your mind and ask for what you want?
■ Do you find it difficult to stand up for yourself in a discussion?

- **Are you inordinately grateful when someone seeks your opinion and takes it into account?**

If you answer 'yes' to most of these questions, you may need to consider becoming more assertive.

Step one: Choose the right approach

Becoming assertive is all about making choices that meet your needs and the needs of the situation. Sometimes it's appropriate to be passive. If you were facing a snarling dog, you might not want to provoke an attack by looking for a win-win situation! There may be other occasions when aggression is the answer. However, this is still assertive behaviour as *you*, rather than other people or situations, are in control of how you react.

TOP TIP

After a lifetime of being the way they are, some people are daunted by the prospect of change. But if you don't change what you do, you'll never change what you get. All it takes to change is a decision. Once you have made that decision, you will naturally observe yourself in situations, notice what you do and don't do well, and then you can try out new behaviours to see what works for you.

✔ You may find it helpful to investigate some specially tailored training courses so that you can try out some approaches before taking on a colleague or manager in a 'live' situation. Assertiveness does not develop overnight: it takes time, practice, and patience.

Step two: Practise projecting a positive image

✔ Use 'winning' language. Rather than saying 'I always come off worst!' say 'I've learned a great deal from doing lots of different things in my career. I'm now ready to move on'. Replacing negative statements with positive affirmations is a simple yet powerful way of taking control in your life.

✔ Visualise yourself how you would like to be. Form a mental image of an assertive you, and then make the image as real as possible, and feel the sensation of being in control. Perhaps there have been moments in your life when you naturally felt like this, a time when you have excelled.

Recapture that moment and 'live' it again. Imagine how it would be if you felt like that in other areas of your life. Determine to make this your goal and recall this powerful image or feeling when you are getting disheartened. It will re-energise you and keep you on track.

TOP TIP

**If you are small in stature, it's easy to think
you can't have presence because people
will overlook you. But many of the
most successful people in business
and in entertainment are physically
quite small. Adopting an assertive
communication style and body
language has the effect of making
you look more imposing. Assume
you have impact, visualise it,
feel it, breathe it.**

Step three: Condition others to take you seriously

This can be done through non-verbal as well as verbal communication.

✔ If someone is talking over you and you're finding it difficult to get a word in edgeways, you can hold up your hand signalling 'stop' as you begin to speak. 'I hear what you are saying but I would like to put forward an alternative viewpoint . . . '

✔ Always take responsibility for your communication. Use the 'I' word. 'I would like . . . ', 'I don't agree . . . ', 'I am uncomfortable with this . . . '

✔ Being aware of non-verbal communication signals can also help you build rapport. If you mirror what others are doing when they are communicating with you, it will help you get a sense of where they are coming from and how to respond in the most helpful way.

TOP TIP
Until you get used to being assertive, you may find it hard to say 'no' to people. One useful technique is to say, 'I'd like to think about this first. I'll get back to you shortly.' Giving yourself time and space to rehearse your response can be really helpful.

Step four: Use positive body language

✔ Stand tall, breathe deeply, and look people in the eye when you speak to them.

✔ Instead of anticipating the negative outcome, expect something positive.

✔ Listen actively to the other party and try putting yourself in their shoes so that you have a better chance of seeking the solution that works for you both.

✔ Inquire about their thoughts and feelings by using 'open' questions that allow them to give you a full response rather than just 'yes' or 'no'. Examples include: 'Tell me more about why . . . ', 'How do you see this working out? . . . ', and 'What are your thoughts on . . . ?'

✔ Don't let people talk down to you when you're sitting down. If they're standing, stand up too!

Step five: Recognise different communication styles

There are four types of communication style:

■ **passive/aggressive**—where you lose and do everything you can (without being too obvious) to make others lose too
■ **passive**—where you lose and everyone else wins
■ **aggressive**—where you win and everyone else loses
■ **assertive**—where everyone wins

It's important to appreciate that people communicate in a variety of ways. Your assertiveness therefore needs to be sensitive to a range of possible responses. Here are some tips on how to deal with the different communication styles outlined above:

✔ **Passive/aggressive people.** If you are dealing with someone behaving in a passive/aggressive manner, you can handle it by exposing what he or she is doing.

'I get the feeling you are not happy about this decision' or 'It appears you have something to say on this; would you like to share your views now?' In this way, they either have to deny their passive/aggressive stance or they have to disclose their motivations. Either way, you are left in the driving seat.

✔ **Passive people.** If you are dealing with a passive person, rather than let them be silent, encourage them to contribute so that they can't put the blame for their disquiet on someone else.

✔ **Aggressive people.** When confronting an aggressive communicator, try not to let the situation get out of hand. One option is to start by saying 'I'd like to think about it first': this gives you time to gather your thoughts and the other person time to calm down. When you're feeling put upon, it's important to remember that you have as much right as anyone to speak up and be heard.

Conflict is notorious for bringing out aggression in people. However, it is still possible to be assertive in this context. You may need to show that you are taking them seriously by reflecting their energy. To do this, you could raise your voice to match the volume of theirs, then bring the volume down as you start to explore what would lead to a win-win solution. 'I CAN SEE THAT YOU ARE UPSET and I would feel exactly the same if I were you . . . however . . . ' Then you can establish the desired outcome for both of you.

If you become more assertive, people won't necessarily think that you have become more aggressive. Be responsive to their communication styles, and their needs will be met too. All that will happen is that your communication style will become more effective.

TOP TIP
Once you become assertive, your confidence levels will be boosted, yet you need to have sufficient levels of confidence to try it in the first place. If you feel you lack the confidence to confront people, try the technique out in a safe environment first so that you get used to how it feels, then you can start to use it more widely.

Common mistakes

✗ You go too far at first
Many people, when trying out assertive behaviour for the first time, find that they go too far and become aggressive. Remember that you are looking for a win-win, not a you-win-and-they-lose situation. Take your time. Observe yourself in action. Practise and ask for feedback from trusted friends or colleagues.

✗ Others react negatively to your assertiveness
Your familiar circle of friends will be used to you the way you were, not the way you want to become. They may try

and make things difficult for you. With your new assertive behaviour, this won't be possible unless you choose it. If you find you're in this situation, try explaining what you're aiming to do and ask for their support. If they're not prepared to help you, you may wish to choose to let them go from your circle of friends.

STEPS TO SUCCESS

✔ Try to avoid feeling resentful—if you are feeling 'put upon', act on it!

✔ Remember that sometimes passivity is the best approach. Don't mistake aggressiveness for assertiveness!

✔ Speaking positively and using positive body language will encourage others to take you seriously and help you to feel you're taking control.

✔ It's important to listen carefully to other people's opinions so you are clear about which points you differ on, and which points you agree on.

✔ Try your techniques out in a safe environment until you feel comfortable with them.

✔ Build up a toolkit of assertive techniques and responses that have worked for you in the past and reuse them.

Useful links

Assertiveness.com:

www.assertiveness.com

Assertiveness tip sheet, Tufts University:

www.tufts.edu/hr/tips/assert.html

The Oak Tree Counseling Self-Help Assertiveness Quiz:

www.theoaktree.com/assrtquz.htm

Developing presence

Presence is an elusive human quality that mysteriously enables someone to command respect, or at least attention. Individuals with presence seem to assert themselves effortlessly.

Some people believe you are born with presence; others, that it develops as a by-product of success. In fact, it is probably a combination of the two—and almost anyone can nurture and develop it.

Presence most often stems from confidence in what you're doing, when you feel most at home with, or passionate about, your role. Conversely, it's most likely to elude you when you feel uncomfortable or unsure of yourself.

Step one: Make yourself comfortable

It's important that you are physically comfortable with how you appear and how you feel. Here are the main areas to focus on when considering how to manage your body.

1 Health and fitness

✔ Look after your physical wellbeing through exercise, a good diet, proper rest, and relaxation techniques such as yoga or meditation.

2 Clothes

✔ Wear clothes you feel comfortable in and that fit well in order to help your posture and improve your confidence. They don't have to be expensive or conventional, just carefully chosen to suit the occasion.

3 Body language

✔ Look for opportunities to project a 'bigger' persona with your physical behaviour. By being aware of and controlling your mannerisms, movements, and demeanour, you are shaping the impact that your presence has on other people. See the box below for some key aspects of body language.

Body language points

✔ **Watch your posture**. Good posture is a great way of increasing your presence and stature. By standing and moving well, you project confidence and calm.

✔ **Maintain steady eye contact**. By making good eye contact with people, whether engaging with them individually or as an audience, you create an impression of honesty, confidence, and directness.

✔ **Demonstrate you are listening**. Paying attention to what people say and showing that you have heard their comments is important. So, too, is remembering people, and the context in which you know them. A useful tip for remembering someone's name is to repeat it when you are introduced, or to use it once or twice in conversation. An audience will pay more attention to you if they feel that you're paying attention to them in return.

✔ **Use appropriate gestures**. Fuller, sweeping arm gestures, rather than small hand movements or pointing fingers, will make a more positive impression. You don't want to overdo it, though, so try rehearsing in front of a mirror first.

It's a good idea to practise all these things, especially if you often feel nervous as a public speaker. A great way to begin would be to give a presentation on a subject that you feel passionate about.

TOP TIP

You can create an impression of being larger than you actually are by using the space around you. For example, when sitting, you might have one arm resting on the back of the chair, your body at an angle, and one leg crossed over the other. This position takes up a large amount of space and is very confident and imposing.

Step two: Prepare your mind

Your mind is one of the most important tools for creating presence. It can create a positive impression—on you as well as others—purely by imagining an idea. Here are some techniques you can use:

1 Visualisation

Our thoughts always precede our actions and behaviour so, by making an intention clear in your mind, you will already be influencing the way you create it in reality. This is the power of positive thinking.

✔ Try to visualise yourself as a person who emanates presence. For example, if you have to make a presentation, first picture the situation in your head and look at it in detail. Examine the feelings you get as you imagine the sound of an audience applauding, and the glow of achievement as you make your exit.

2 The 'anchor' technique

If, as many people find, you perform well in one situation but not in another, your mind can help here too.

✔ Think of a situation in which you feel comfortable or of some activity that you know you are really good at. Then link that feeling to a gesture, movement, or saying—such as pinching your thumb and forefinger together. This becomes the 'anchor', and when you repeat your anchor in a new setting, all the memories of performing well will flood back and help you to do so again.

TOP TIP

A common problem is to feel that the presence and credibility you have with junior colleagues disappears in front of your managers and peers. With junior colleagues, you have three things that they don't: knowledge, expertise, and authority. Your peers and managers probably do have the same or more of these things—or they create the illusion that they do—and this can be sufficiently intimidating to make you lose your confidence. Try the 'anchor' technique to help you carry the confidence you feel with junior colleagues into situations with your managers and peers.

---

3 Positive affirmations

By telling yourself 'I am confident', 'I feel good', 'I have presence', you can subconsciously begin to influence your outward behaviour.

✔ Repeat your positive affirmations regularly so that they become the dominant messages you transmit about yourself.

TOP TIP
When repeating positive affirmations to yourself, make sure they are in the present tense. If you say, 'I *will* be confident', your brain will believe it to be a *future* scenario—and you may never get there!

Step three: Know what you know

It's important to acknowledge your areas of expertise. These are the topics that you feel you have mastered and that you're therefore most comfortable addressing. Remember that you have useful things to say and that people want to hear them.

✔ Use the knowledge and experience you have built up over the years to practise being confident in what you say and do. Make sure that people know your worth by being open and honest: share your experiences, tell stories, and engage people at a human level.

Bear in mind that you're not the only person who needs to have their presence acknowledged. People on a mission to assert their presence often stop seeing and listening to others.

✔ Try to be inclusive, and a reputation for 'generosity' will also become part of your presence.

Step four: Create the occasion

Projecting presence demands an occasion. This may be any type of event, from a one-to-one interview, to a gathering of a few people, or a formal presentation to a large audience. People with presence are able to create a sense of occasion in even the most ordinary of circumstances, such as walking along the production line, chairing a meeting, or giving a presentation.

✔ Think through your dramatic strategy, and practise so that you get the timing and pace right.

Projecting presence is a responsibility. Presence is about transmitting a quality that others trust and respond to. It makes them feel as if they are gaining something just from being close to you. For those who look up to you, you will be providing guidance and inspiring confidence, reflecting their values, and—perhaps—being their conscience.

✔ It's important that you are fully committed to your desire for presence, and not pursuing a power trip!

Common mistakes

✗ **You mistake over-confidence for presence**
As developing presence is closely linked to developing self-confidence, it's all too easy to overstep the line and come across as self-interested and over-confident.

Ironically, the very people who show over-confidence are often those most lacking in confidence, and they may be trying to compensate for this. But it's important to remember that part of developing presence is taking an interest in and building relationships with other people.

✗ You think presence cannot be developed
Some people are born with a certain amount of natural presence. Nevertheless, it's a gift that needs attention and development to mature properly. Look for occasions where you can practise the techniques that will help you project the impression you seek. In time, it will become second nature.

✗ You aren't fully prepared
Although there are four steps involved in creating presence, it's important to have an organic approach to them all. It's no use looking good, having a clear intention, and creating the occasion—but having nothing to say. Or conversely, imagine having a great story or piece of information, but getting the timing all wrong. Each element assists and supports the others, so you need to pay careful attention to them all.

STEPS TO SUCCESS

✔ Take care of your physical wellbeing.

✔ Dress comfortably and appropriately to the occasion.

✔ Build up physical confidence.

✔ Use the space around you to create a bigger persona.

✔ Visualise positive scenarios and how it feels to emanate presence.

✔ Use gestures or sayings as 'anchors' — transferable markers that you associate with doing something really well.

✔ Repeat positive affirmations about yourself.

✔ Be confident in the things that you know.

✔ Be aware of those around you.

✔ Create a sense of occasion.

Mastering all these elements will open new doors of opportunity for you: people will gravitate to you, offer you new leadership roles, and spread the good word about your qualities and skills.

Useful links

Impactfactory.com:
www.impactfactory.com/snacks.shtml
Pertinent.com:
www.pertinent.com/articles/communication/index.asp

Building confidence at work

Confidence is a cornerstone of assertiveness. For those who are blessed with it, it's unremarkable. For those who do not have it, it's an extraordinarily difficult quality to develop and sustain.

We all have moments when our confidence blossoms—when we feel good about ourselves, have the knowledge we need to overcome any doubts, and are able to achieve any goal, however large or small. So we know what we are missing when confidence is lacking and, in the act of noticing its absence, we diminish the possibility of bringing it back to the surface.

Fear is the main emotion that undermines confidence. We can become flustered purely by the 'what if' scenarios that we conjure up in our minds. It is this irrational fear that needs to be addressed because, until it is dealt with, you won't have the confidence to assert yourself fully.

Step one: Know your job

Confidence cannot be put on like a coat—it has to be rooted firmly in the psyche. If you play-act at having confidence, it comes across as empty or brash. It may help you get through a situation, but it won't fuel the development of this quality in the longer term. Unfortunately, building confidence requires hard work.

Confidence comes from knowing what to do, how to do it, and when to do it. This know-how may be learned in a college or university setting, or it may have been developed on the job. Knowledge allows you to work within clear boundaries of competence. You will then become recognised for your abilities, reinforcing your self-image and building your confidence.

✔ If you are put into a different job where you don't have the same level of familiarity, your confidence may be shaken. In this case, focus first on your transferable skills before developing the other abilities you will require.

TOP TIP
People often lose their confidence when promoted or transferred, and many are tempted to go back to their old comfort zone. If a return route is not open to them, they may try superimposing familiar habits onto their new role. If you are suffering this kind of anxiety, ask for feedback or coaching to enable you to expand your skills and build the confidence you need to succeed.

Step two: Establish clear objectives

Confidence often increases with success, and success can only be proven when a goal or objective has been reached. Clear objectives allow you to monitor your progress and adjust your focus in order to achieve your aims.

✔ Don't be afraid to ask for targets from your manager. Without this level of clarity, you could be prevented from enjoying success because no one has defined success in that context. Without objectives—and therefore without successes—people's enthusiasm and level of energy diminish, along with their confidence.

✔ Make sure your targets are clearly defined so that your criteria for success are unambiguous. Poorly articulated objectives cause more personal grief in organisations than almost anything else. It's incredibly disconcerting to find that you are pouring energy into a professional void.

Step three: Unite authority and accountability

Nothing is more disheartening than taking the blame for something that is not your fault. Such knock-backs are damaging to confidence and motivation. Being accountable for failure without having the authority to make decisions can be extremely stressful.

✔ Talk to your boss and colleagues in order to define the boundaries and responsibilities of your role. You may need to explain that this is not an attempt to avoid accountability, but rather an initiative to clarify your goals and thereby focus your efforts.

✔ Confidence comes from a job well done, so make sure that your stated objectives are dependent on your own performance, not that of others. If you are accountable for a project, you will take full credit for its success—and you will also be more motivated to make sure things run smoothly.

TOP TIP
Don't worry if you fall short of your targets at first. If you show improvement, your progress will be recognised. Always keep your results in perspective and take heart in your development.

Step four: Work on your personal development

Many organisations these days place responsibility for learning and development on the employee. However, it's worth reminding your employer that if you improve your skills, the company will benefit too. When a business invests in its people, it has a very positive effect on employees' confidence and their ability to contribute to the organisation's success.

✔ Enquire about your company's policy on training. It may even be mentioned in your employment contract. You might find that they offer assistance you weren't aware of. Organisational support is often given in the form of advice, mentoring, time off for study, or participation in special projects.

✔ Learning and development should be jointly planned and agreed upon by you and your organisation. This way, your new skills will be tailored to suit your job.

✔ Explore the options. External training programmes may be the appropriate solution, especially when there are specialist skills or areas of knowledge that need to be developed.

TOP TIP
One of the essential ingredients of confidence is good communication. If you feel that you can communicate effectively in any situation—conveying thoughts to colleagues, building rapport with difficult clients, getting through to senior management, and so on—your level of confidence will be high. It is therefore worth considering a course that will develop your communication skills.

Step five: Celebrate

Celebrations are very important. They are a way of acknowledging that an objective has been achieved and rewarding those responsible. They generate enthusiasm, build confidence, and boost morale.

A celebration can be as simple as a selection of cakes during coffee break; or it might be as elaborate as a large function to celebrate the achievement of organisational objectives or exceptional year-end results.

Although some people are internally driven—they don't need external recognition to make them feel as though they have succeeded—most people value some form of public appreciation.

✔ Make sure that you and your team celebrate your achievements. If necessary, remind your bosses of the value of celebrations and persuade them to participate. If the successes are relatively small, you can still organise your own festivities.

✔ The prospect of a celebration can be a strong motivating factor. The thought of a bottle of champagne can be much more of an incentive than its cash value would suggest.

✔ The memory of a celebration will inspire confidence and enthusiasm in future projects.

TOP TIP
Public recognition not only validates your
contribution but also increases your visibility,
reinforcing your confidence and enhancing
your opportunities for promotion and
advancement.

Common mistakes

✗ You fail to delegate

Many managers feel the burden of accountability so
heavily that they no longer have the confidence to
delegate. They feel that allowing their people the
freedom to make decisions will result in a loss of control.
Due to this fear, they control the decision-making, and
alienate their team in the process. Keeping strict control
can actually disable the team and undermine the
confidence they have in their own abilities. This will
subsequently affect results and dent your own
confidence.

✗ You become dependent

If you are lucky enough to have a mentor or a supportive
boss, you can become dependent on their advice. This
is particularly common after promotion. You may well
have the skills to do the job, but after a while, you can
lose the confidence to make your own decisions.
Perhaps your mentor has contributed to this problem

by being too protective or not giving you enough freedom. You will have to wean yourself off their expertise. Raise this issue with them and identify areas or projects that you can begin managing without support.

✗ You fear the worst

Rather than concentrate on what you can control, you allow your mind to entertain thoughts of disaster. Confidence comes from doing what you do well, so focus on your core skills. Get the basics right and minor problems will not be significant. If you have clearly defined areas of accountability, you should be able to anticipate and overcome any worrying issues.

STEPS TO SUCCESS

✔ Know which skills you need to do your job. If you lack some of them, ask for advice or training.

✔ Make sure you have clearly defined targets. Set yourself personal goals if necessary.

✔ Take control of your work. Ensure that you are not accountable for results over which you have no authority.

✔ Seek out opportunities for training. Confidence comes from knowledge and skills.

✔ Celebrate your achievements, to build confidence and raise your profile.

Useful links

BBC Health:

www.bbc.co.uk/health/confidence/learn

More-SelfEsteem.com:

www.more-selfesteem.com

Self-confidence.co.uk:

www.self-confidence.co.uk/self/confidence/tips.html

Managing others' perceptions

We all hold differing views of the world, partly because of our different cultural backgrounds, life experiences, and personal values. Naturally, these influence the way we interact with one another. Our behaviours, competences, style, and approach further affect our relationships.

However, we are not entirely products of our past—we are consciously capable of modifying our conduct and, in turn, affecting the impression we make on others. Learning how to project a positive image of ourselves can be an invaluable tool in many areas of our lives, but especially in the workplace.

In senior management roles, it is particularly important to understand and manage the way we are regarded.

This is not as difficult as you might think. Although it requires a good deal of thought, motivation, and self-awareness, with practice you'll soon find it easier to assert your personality, motivate people, and lead them in a desired direction.

Step one: Overcome your misgivings

1 It's not about deception

Some people feel that changing the way you are perceived is a form of deception; they believe it involves pretending you are something you're not. However, managing perceptions is more about shedding light on your positive aspects while minimising the visibility of your weaknesses. It's not about deceit. It's about letting your true talents shine through.

2 It's a part of life

We live in a culture where people and organisations spend enormous sums of money hiring others to manage perceptions. The same skills used by advertising and public relations companies can be employed by you to influence those around you.

✔ Be aware of the impression your behaviour creates. This is the first step towards perception management. Gradually, you can develop skills that help you to manage your behaviour in a way that will move your career forward in the direction you want.

3 It can help you in your career

In the modern employment market, there is a greater onus on autonomy. Careers are no longer managed by organisations, but are directed by individuals themselves. You are judged not only on what you do, but on how you do it—so evaluation by others now plays an important role in your career. People who can manage perceptions are likely to receive more offers and find fewer obstacles in their career path.

TOP TIP
Take care of your relationships as you move up the career ladder, because you may encounter the same people later when you are moving back down! People can harbour grudges for years, and you don't want to risk encountering an unforgiving individual in a position of influence. If you find it impossible to change your attitude, you'd better have skills that make you indispensable!

Step two: Understand how you are perceived

To understand how others view you, you must have an accurate understanding of yourself. Building self-awareness requires courage, commitment, and forgiveness.

✔ Firstly, encourage informal feedback from trusted peers and managers. Remember that people will be giving you *their* opinions and these may not resonate with you—you may be surprised at the way you are perceived. Try to remain objective and find out where these views have come from.

✔ Use more formal tools that enable you to understand yourself, such as psychometric tests and personality profiles. The feedback from these is sometimes easier to manage because it's objective and has no third party involvement.

✔ Sometimes, 360-degree surveys are used to gather the views of different audiences, both inside and outside the business. These tend to focus on behaviour and competence. Be aware of the differences between the two. While both may be learned and modified, changing behaviour usually involves altering personality traits and perceptions and may be more difficult than acquiring new skills.

✔ When reviewing test results, try not to concentrate solely on personal information that is hurtful. Look for patterns in the feedback, and reflect on when and why these may have arisen. Pressure can often allow unintentional behaviour to come to the surface and this may have given rise to impressions that you would like to change.

TOP TIP
People generally hold onto first impressions, and it can be difficult to replace them with something more to your liking. Changing how others view you requires a consistent flow of new messages, and this means persistent awareness and self-evaluation—both of which take time and energy to develop.

Step three: Determine your strategy

Before embarking on any perception management strategy, establish what your goals are, how you are going to reach them, and how you will track your success.

✔ Don't be too ambitious at first: focus on one thing you can change that will create an immediate impression.

✔ Think of the context in which you are working, and use your feedback to select your initial goals.

Do

- Increase your own awareness.
- Be aware of your impact on others and interpret the signals they transmit to you.
- Be aware of the effect of pressure on you and how this looks to others.
- Be visible at strategic moments.
- Gently encourage feedback from people whose opinions you value.
- Allow others to have their choices.
- Give yourself time to change.
- Be consistent, patient, and forgiving of yourself and others.

Don't

- React emotionally to the feedback you receive.

- Get defensive.
- Become de-motivated.
- Become sycophantic.
- Get too big for your boots and try too hard too quickly.
- Expect too much.
- Embroil others in your views of yourself.
- Pester people for feedback.
- Be political or manipulative in your behaviour.

In a nutshell, perception management is all about creating an impression through conscious activities and awareness of your audience and the impact you have upon them. To succeed, you must:

✔ define your target audience

✔ be conscious of their values

✔ adjust your communication style

✔ encourage feedback

✔ be aware of how you adjust and adapt your behaviours

Step four: Gather support

While there may be encouragement to change your behaviour initially, remember that there may also be reactions to those changes. People are accustomed to the 'old' you and may have difficulty adjusting to the 'new' you. It is therefore important to do four things.

✓ Communicate your intentions to people who may be affected. If you have a formal annual performance appraisal, make it a 'learning objective', as this is likely to win more support and forgiveness if things don't work out quite the way you wish. You will also receive more praise when you are successful.

✓ Gain support from your manager or key members of your team to help keep you focused. A good support group is essential when seeking to change something about yourself. Extraordinary transformations have been achieved with the help of groups such as Alcoholics Anonymous and Weight Watchers.

✓ Find a coach to provide ongoing guidance. A coach will be able to offer impartial observations and encourage you to continue, or change, your strategy as you move forward. Coaching takes time and commitment, so you will need to allow for this in your work plan.

✓ Evaluate your progress at each milestone in your plan, either formally or informally. It is important to gather informal feedback regularly, but make sure you give people enough time to observe your new behaviour before asking for their opinions. You might warn those whom you are going to approach for feedback, so they can consciously pay attention to your behaviour. A more formal option is to revisit the 360-degree questionnaire and see whether others have noticed the change.

Don't lose heart if the changes in your approach are not immediately recognised by others. It may take months, so consistency and perseverance are essential.

TOP TIP
If you wish to change someone's impression of you, you must first understand both that person's existing perception and the one you wish to create. You then need to create a bridge between the two. Observe the person's values and behaviour and find an opportunity to convey a different message. However, you must be honest in the way you portray yourself. If you create an impression that is not essentially *you* the deception will be easy to spot, simply because living a lie is extraordinarily difficult to sustain.

Common mistakes

✗ You become impatient
It's easy to be impatient for results and give up too quickly. Behavioural change is not as easy as learning

a new skill; it requires dedication, commitment, and consistency. It is only through constant repetition and reinforcement of your new behaviour that people's perceptions will change.

✗ You don't ask for feedback

Some people are embarrassed to ask for feedback and help, particularly when they are in senior roles. This is because many forms of behaviour are habitual, and some may even have contributed to previous promotions. However, conduct appropriate to some roles may not be right for others. Promotion to a management position can highlight these differences, when relationships suddenly become much more important than technical skills. In this situation, use a new project or a particular aspect of your new role as a test-bed for the new you.

✗ You aim too high

In trying to change behaviours, people can be too ambitious and therefore lose the support of others. While it's important to be enthusiastic, try to understate rather than overstate your goals. It's always easier to deal with the surprise of your audience, rather than their disappointment.

STEPS TO SUCCESS

✔ Acknowledge the importance of perception management.

✔ Find out how people perceive you and how that differs from your own perception.

✔ Start small: begin by changing only one aspect of your image.

✔ Define your target audience, align your values with theirs, and adjust your communication style accordingly.

✔ Encourage feedback and involve other people in helping you sustain the change.

✔ Don't expect too much too soon.

Useful links

Alinea Group:
**www.alineagroup.com/
Impression%20Management.htm**
All About Human Resources:
http://humanresources.about.com
Global Image Group:
www.globalimagegrp.com
Perception Rules:
www.perceptionrules.net

Using non-verbal communication

Non-verbal communication involves many different 'channels' that convey meaning beyond what is being said. These include gestures, body movement, facial expressions, and even vocal tone and pitch. It's not an exact science, although we sometimes make judgments as if it were.

It's widely understood that the majority of information is conveyed through non-verbal signals, most of which come from the eyes. This explains why it's often hard to convey subtle meanings over the telephone or through the written word. Because the person receiving your message can't see your body or face, your meaning may well be misinterpreted.

If you can learn to employ non-verbal channels consciously, you will add a new dimension to your persuasive skills, enabling you to build rapport and assert your opinions to much greater effect. In addition, as part of the learning process, you will also develop skills that will enable you to read and interpret the non-verbal communication of others.

Step one: Match and mirror

If you watch two people talking in a relaxed and unself-conscious manner, you may notice that their bodies have taken on a similar demeanour. Both may have crossed their legs, or settled into their chairs in similar postures. If they are eating or drinking, they may do so at the same rate. This is called *matching* or *mirroring*, and it occurs naturally between two people who feel that they're on the same wavelength.

✔ Matching and mirroring can be used consciously as a technique to achieve rapport with someone, but you need to be subtle. Exaggerated mirroring looks like mimicry, and the other person is likely to feel embarrassed or angry.

TOP TIP
Even with a large audience, you can still build rapport. Suppose you are addressing a group of professionals from a podium. Make sure you seek information from everyone, acknowledge every contribution, give anyone who hesitates plenty of space, and support anyone who finds it difficult to speak in front of a group. If there are too many people in the room to pay attention to each one, invite contributions from those who are most extrovert and build rapport with them. This will give others confidence in your ability to connect with people.

✔ Observe what your counterparts do with their bodies as they're talking. Then follow the pattern of their non-verbal communication and reflect it back. Once this feels natural, try to take the lead by changing your body position and watch to see if they follow. You may well find that more often than not they do.

Once you begin to get a feel for this process, see if you can use it in a situation that is problematic. Perhaps there is someone at work with whom you do not have a good rapport. See if you can lead that person into a more relaxed exchange by practising the matching and mirroring technique.

TOP TIP
Sometimes, you might inadvertently convey the wrong message—perhaps you have a habit of using an expression or gesture that is commonly accepted to mean one thing when you really mean something different. A nervous laugh, for example, might indicate that you think you're being funny. You may, in fact, be trying to communicate something serious, but are nervous because the subject is a bit delicate. Training can help correct the most obvious quirks in your non-verbal lexicon. In the meantime it might help to acknowledge your idiosyncrasies publicly so people don't get the wrong impression.

Step two: Speak the same language

Neurolinguistic programming (NLP)

According to NLP (a method of tapping into the unconscious mind to reveal what is going on beneath the surface), language can indicate a great deal about how an individual views the world. Depending on which of the five senses they subconsciously favour, people may fall into one of five noticeable types:

- visual (sight)
- auditory (hearing)
- kinaesthetic (touch)
- olfactory (smell)
- gustatory (taste)

You can establish rapport with people more effectively by paying attention to their individual preferences for 'sensual' cues.

✔ When talking to someone you don't know well, listen to the kinds of words he or she uses. Once you have identified which of the five categories (see above) they belong to, respond by using the same kind of language. See the list on the next two pages for examples of some of the words to look out for.

In other words, when you are building rapport with someone, using the same kind of language is a subtle way of significantly enhancing the level of understanding between you.

Different types of vocabulary

Here are some examples of words and expressions that can help you identify the five different types of people:

- **visual language** includes terms like *see*, *appear*, *show*, *clear*, *picture*, *focused*, *well-defined*, *in light of*, *dim view*, *get a perspective on*, and *looks like*. For example, a person might say something like, 'I have a *vision* of what this organisation will *look* like in five year's time. I can *see* that it will take lots of energy to create what is in my *mind's eye*'. You can respond similarly: 'You build a very *clear picture* for me. I can *see* that this will be a challenge, but your *farsightedness* will surely enable you to reach your *dream*'.
- **auditory language** includes terms like *hear*, *listen*, *tune in/out*, *rumour*, *sound*, *clear as a bell*, *unheard of*, *word for word*, and *be all ears*. An auditory person might say, 'I *hear* that you have been promoted. You must have done a *resoundingly* good job!' You could respond, 'Yes, I have been *called* upon to *sound* out the market and *ring* some changes in the way we sell our products'.

- **kinaesthetic language** includes terms like *sense*, *feel*, *move towards*, *grasp*, *get hold of*, *solid*, *make contact*, *touch*, *concrete*, *pull some strings*, and *sensitive*.
- **olfactory language** includes terms like *smell*, *odour*, *rotten*, *aromatic*, and *fragrance*, and expressions like *turn your nose up* and *sniff out*.
- **gustatory language** includes terms like *bitter*, *sweet*, *sour*, *salty* and other taste-related words.

Step three: Listen actively

Active listening is a rare skill, but it is very effective in helping you build rapport with other people. It can also yield valuable information, enabling us to do our jobs more efficiently.

✔ Demonstrate that you have understood and are interested in what is being said in conversation. This kind of active listening requires good eye contact, lots of head nods, and responses such as 'Ah ha', 'Mmmm', and 'I understand what you mean'.

✔ Summarise what has been said to demonstrate your understanding, and ask open questions such as, 'Can you tell me more about . . . ?' and 'What do you think . . . ?'. These questions encourage further communication and enrich what is being communicated.

TOP TIP
People often try to cover up anger at work.
However, their tone of voice, subtle changes
in facial expression, and aggressive gestures
are likely to convey their real emotions. For
example, maybe someone will start pacing
up and down or banging the table while
still smiling pleasantly in an attempt to
hide their true but socially unacceptable
feelings. Active listening and open
questions can help to defuse anger
before it boils over.

Step four: Interpret in context

Much has been written about non-verbal communication,
especially about how to read body language. This may give
you insight into what is going on, but always remember to
place your interpretation in context. For example, someone
sitting in a meeting with his or her arms crossed is possibly
being aggressive, reluctant, or disapproving. But, perhaps
the person is shy, cold, or ill.

✔ Be cautious of jumping to conclusions about how
someone is feeling without further information.

If you move to a new environment with a different work
culture, there could be a risk of misunderstandings at a
non-verbal level. Perhaps your new boss is more emotional

than your previous manager and expects a more energetic display of your enthusiasm for the job.

✔ Make sure you take time to observe what is going on around you and note how the different context makes you feel. Perhaps ask advice from someone in the new culture who shares something of your own experience—they may be able to provide a useful communications bridge.

✔ In the first few weeks in your new work environment, beware of jumping to over-hasty conclusions based purely on non-verbal signals.

TOP TIP

Non-verbal messages can help you spot when someone is lying. Usually, when people are communicating in a straightforward way, their non-verbal signals are consistent with their words: they might say, 'I'm unhappy about that', and their face and body will droop too. When people are bluffing, their gestures are usually inconsistent with their speech. Someone may say, 'The deal is almost in the bag!'—but you notice a nervous body pattern, like the shifting of feet or the tapping of fingers. Unusual avoidance of eye contact or blinking can also indicate an inconsistency, which communication experts call *leakage*.

Common mistakes

✗ **You lack subtlety**

People new to the techniques of non-verbal communication can be over-enthusiastic practitioners. Observe yourself objectively to make sure you aren't offending others by broadly mimicking their speech or behaviour. Remember that most people instinctively send and interpret non-verbal signals all the time: don't assume you're the only one who's aware of non-verbal undercurrents. Finally, stay true to yourself. Be aware of your own natural style, and don't adopt behaviours that are incompatible with it.

✗ **You ignore context**

Putting too much store by someone's non-verbal signals can lead to misinterpretation and misunderstandings. It's important to understand the context in which the signals are being transmitted and think through the possible scenarios before jumping in.

✗ **You over-emphasise non-verbal signals**

Trying to control your meaning by emphasising your non-verbal signals can make you look ill at ease. It is very difficult to convey convincing messages that do not genuinely reflect what you think. Even if it is very subtle, leakage is bound to occur. This will raise people's suspicions and level of distrust. The best way to build rapport using non-verbal cues is to be authentic in what

you say, and your body language will reinforce that
message naturally.

STEPS TO SUCCESS

✔ Watch the body language of others and mirror it if you
wish to build rapport. Use your own body language to
influence tense situations and lead people into more
relaxed exchanges.

✔ Observe the language used by those you wish to
influence, listening out for 'sensual' cues. Enhance the
level of understanding between you by tailoring your
own choice of words to complement theirs.

✔ Listen attentively and actively: keep reassuring the other
person that you're not just listening, but that you're
interested in what he or she has to say.

✔ Think carefully before interpreting non-verbal signals,
especially in a new and unfamiliar environment—there
could be many reasons for unusual behaviour.

✔ Look out for leakage: non-verbal signals that either
contradict or don't match what the person is saying. It
can help you identify when someone is hiding
something.

✔ Remember that other people know about these
techniques and will be able to spot any obvious attempts
to influence their opinions. Be subtle!

Useful links

NLP training and resources:

www.altfeld.com/mastery/seminars/desc-sb1.html

The non-verbal dictionary of gestures, signs, and body language:

http://members.aol.com/nonverbal2/diction1.htm

PPI Business NLP:

www.ppimk.com

Rider University Clinical Psychology Department:

www.rider.edu/users/suler/bodylang.html

Dealing with stressful relationships and bullying

It can be very hard to assert yourself in the workplace if you have a difficult or challenging relationship with a more dominant colleague— particularly when it's with your boss. It can be tempting to lay the blame for this type of situation at the other person's feet, due to his or her unreasonable, negative, awkward, or unhelpful behaviour. Whether justified or not, the good news is that there is plenty that you can do to change the dynamic of the relationship.

Abusive behaviour ranges from the extreme, such as bullying and physical abuse, to more subtle forms of harassment that are often more common but less recognised. What is tolerated in the workplace will depend very much upon the culture of the organisation and the attitudes of its leaders. Some businesses ignore all forms of harassment; others make a point of creating a culture where intimidation of any sort is cause for reprimand or dismissal.

It is worth reflecting on your organisation's culture to see what maltreatment exists, both on and under the surface.

Step one: Understand the forms bullying can take

The recipient of bullying is often in a weaker position, physically, emotionally, or hierarchically. Victims are usually unable or unwilling to stand up for themselves, due to what they feel will be the unacceptable consequences, such as an escalation of abusive behaviour or the threat of redundancy. This fear allows the behaviour to continue.

Any form of harassment can have a serious impact on the morale of staff in the business, and can affect the performance and health of individuals. Not only is it damaging, but it's also unlawful, and should be treated seriously.

Different forms of harassment

These include:

- all manner of physical contact from touching, pushing, and shoving, to serious assault
- intrusive or obsessive behaviour, such as constant pestering, baiting, or dogging a person's movements
- tricks being played that result in risk or danger to the individual
- group bullying, where the individual is overpowered by a number of aggressors

Less direct forms of harassment include:

- the spreading of rumours about the individual, making jokes or offensive personal remarks
- written statements, letters, or graffiti
- actions that isolate the individual and prevent them from doing their work effectively
- non co-operation, or sabotage of professional objectives
- pressure for sexual favours
- obscene gestures and comments
- the orchestration of situations that compromise the individual
- manipulative 'political' behaviours, that may include bribery or blackmail

TOP TIP

The difference between a good joke and bullying can be subtle. However, if the person being bullied is demeaned and disempowered in some way, or if the joke becomes personally critical and destructive, then the line has been crossed. It's important to remember that it's not the intention of the person playing the joke that determines whether the line has been crossed, it's the feelings it provokes in the victim.

Step two: Recognise the mental and physical impact

If you are being bullied, don't be tempted to live with the difficulties of having a troublesome boss or work colleague, seeking ways to minimise the impact he or she has on your working life. Avoidance tactics can be more time-consuming and stressful than being assertive and confronting the problem.

✔ Focus on your own health as this may encourage you to tackle the issue rationally and try to reach an accommodation that will prevent you from jeopardising your health or feeling that you have to leave your job.

Step three: Determine when the line has been crossed

Often, people find it hard to know whether the line of harassment has been crossed. If they confront the perpetrators, they can be accused of 'being a poor sport', or worse. Such accusations are often levelled to mask what is going on, and can seriously undermine the victim's confidence.

✔ Seek feedback from those who may have observed any incidents. Their account may give you more ammunition to deal with the problem appropriately. Select your witness carefully though—ones you can trust to be allies throughout the ordeal, who won't 'flip' on you under pressure.

Determining whether the harassment is trivial or serious is paramount. If it is infrequent and seems harmless, try not to take it too personally. Remember that bullying says more about the character of the bully than it does about you. However, if the bullying is persistent or escalates, you must confront it and report it. Even if you don't wish to face the bully head on, there are likely to be other ways of asserting your rights.

TOP TIP

If you feel you're being bullied, but the perpetrator disguises his or her actions with jokes, one way of dealing with this is to write down the incidents in a journal, including the context in which they took place. Ask for feedback from observers and include their comments. Over time, you will be able to see if there is a pattern to the treatment you have been receiving. Also, the record may be useful if you decide to take the matter further.

✔ Check in the employees' handbook if you have one. There are probably procedures in place to assist you in dealing with your situation. You may be advised to report

the incident(s) to your manager but, should you feel
uncomfortable about this—for example, if your manager
is part of the problem (see below)—you may wish to go
to the human resources department if you have one.

✔ If you decide to lodge a formal complaint, make sure you
have a record of the incidents and a note of the
witnesses present.

Step four: Deal with a difficult boss

Many people have a challenging relationship with their
boss. When examining such a relationship, it's important
to realise how much of it is due to the structure of the
organisation—your boss necessarily has to give you tasks,
some of which you may not enjoy—and how much is due
to truly unreasonable behaviour. Looking at the wider issues
in the organisation may provide the key to the problem.
Acting upon your discoveries will require a combination of
assertiveness and sensitivity.

I Understand your boss

'Difficult boss syndrome' is rarely caused simply by a
personality clash.

✔ However uncomfortable it may feel, try putting yourself in
your boss's shoes. Recognise the objectives that define
his or her role and think through the pressures they are
under. Make a mental list of your boss's strengths,

preferred working style, idiosyncrasies, values, and beliefs.

This will help you deepen your understanding. Very often, when we feel disliked or when we dislike someone, we avoid building this understanding and instead look for ways of avoiding the issues.

TOP TIP

If your boss is making work intolerable because of his or her moody and bad-tempered behaviour, try to work out how you could influence the situation for the better. Observe his or her behaviour to see if there is a pattern in it, and then try giving constructive feedback, letting your boss know how his or her mood swings affect you. Use assertive language and ask if there is anything you can do to alleviate the cause of the problem. If the behaviour persists, you may wish to consult your human resources department to see if there are any formal procedures in place to deal with such a situation.

---

2 Compare the way you both perceive your role

You may feel that you are performing well, but if you are putting all your energy into completing tasks that your boss does not consider to be relevant or a priority, you will be seen as performing poorly.

✔ Take the initiative to explore your boss's expectations and agree on your objectives. This will clarify your role and give you a better idea of how to progress in the organisation.

TOP TIP
A lack of communication often contributes to workplace misunderstandings. If you feel like you're missing out on opportunities or being denied information because you're not one of your boss's favourites, try approaching him or her with information about what you're doing for a consultation on your methods and goals. If your boss persists in denying you the information you need, you may have a case of bullying against him or her.

---

3 Ask for the support you need

When managers neglect to give their employees the information and support they need, this creates ambiguity and forces employees to second-guess their boss's requirements.

✔ Ask for the information and resources you need. If your boss is not immediately forthcoming, try talking to some of your colleagues or looking around for other ways to access them. This will put you firmly in control of the situation and protect you from the need to improvise.

4 Understand yourself

Sometimes, a lack of self-knowledge may lead to us being surprised by the feedback we get and our reactions to it. In getting to know yourself better, you may wish to ask for input from your colleagues.

✔ Ask your colleagues what they observe when you interact with your boss, how you come across to them, and how you could manage your communication differently. Although their perception may not represent the absolute truth about you, it nonetheless reflects the image you create.

5 Consider changing aspects of your behaviour

This often prompts a reciprocal behavioural change in your boss. If you don't change anything about the way you interact with your boss, the relationship will retain the same dynamics and remain unaltered, so this is definitely worth a try.

✔ Think through some of the past encounters you have had with your boss and reflect upon them objectively, perhaps with a friend or colleague who knows you well.

✔ Identify any recurring patterns in your interactions. Perhaps this situation happens over and over again, which suggests that you harbour a value or belief that is being repeatedly compromised. If you can understand what this is, you can learn to manage these situations more effectively.

Perhaps you value attention to detail, but your boss is a big-picture person. Every time you ask for more detailed information, you will be drawing attention to one of your boss's vulnerabilities, and he or she is likely to become unco-operative or irritated by your request.

Once you have observed your respective patterns, you can work around them or accommodate them dispassionately.

6 Remember that a relationship is mutual
In order to be considered effective, managers need a co-operative and productive team. But in order to be part of such a team, each member needs their manager to provide the resources and support they need to do their job properly.

It's well known that some of the most stressful situations arise when dependents' needs are not met. People find a variety of ways to deal with this. Some become angry and resentful of the manager's authority; some find ways of challenging decisions in order to assert some of their own power; and others become compliant saboteurs. It's rare in business to find relationships where there is absolutely *no* reciprocal power.

7 When all else fails . . .
Remember that if you are no longer willing to spend time managing your difficult boss, you still have the ultimate power: you can just walk away.

TOP TIP
If your boss is making you feel miserable by constantly making negative and derisive comments about the way you do your work, you need to find a private moment when you can explain how this makes you feel and ask your boss to stop doing it. You could suggest that he or she gives you clear guidelines and constructive feedback that will help you to meet his or her expectations and develop your talents. Point out that constant nagging affects the way you work and that you would be much more effective if he or she took a positive interest in what you do.

Common mistakes

✗ **You mistake a genuine extrovert for a bully**
Extroverts frequently speak their minds before really thinking about what they are saying—which can sound confrontational and be mistaken for harassment. Being extroverts, however, they are often receptive to questioning and keen to point out that they were just testing the boundaries, or joking. By sharing your perception and inviting theirs, it's possible to clarify and dispel the situation without further entanglement.

✗ You take your boss's behaviour personally

It is very tempting to take the behaviour of a difficult boss personally. However, it is very unlikely that *you* are the problem. It may be something you do, it may be the values you hold, or it may be that you remind your boss of someone he or she doesn't get on with.

✗ You don't remain detached

Many difficult relationships deteriorate to the point where they are fraught with contempt and confrontation. This is never helpful in a work setting and only makes matters uncomfortable for everyone. If you find yourself being drawn into an angry exchange, try to remain emotionally detached and listen actively to what is being said (or shouted) to you. It may provide you with clues about why the situation has developed and allow you to get straight to the point of concern. Ask for a private review afterwards to explore the incident. This may bring to the surface issues that are relatively easy to deal with and that will prevent further outbursts from occurring.

✗ You never confront the issue

Because facing up to harassment is so difficult, many people avoid biting the bullet. Inactivity will only prolong a miserable situation. Acquiescence enables bullying to thrive and allows the aggressors to maintain the power imbalance. Try taking responsibility for your share of the problem and examine what it is you may be doing to provoke conflict between you and your boss or colleague.

STEPS TO SUCCESS

✔ Be aware that there are many kinds of bullying, most of which do not involve physical abuse. You may be suffering in more ways than you know.

✔ Realise that inactivity is not an option. The only thing you're likely to achieve by doing nothing is endangering your career and jeopardising your health.

✔ Ask others for their opinions on whether your treatment constitutes bullying.

✔ If the line has been crossed, resolve to take action and assert your rights. Select your witnesses carefully and keep a record of the bullying incidences.

✔ Your first step should be to go through formal, established channels rather than confronting the issue on your own.

✔ If your relationship with your boss is problematic, try to see it from both sides and understand why he or she may act the way they do.

✔ You may be able to improve the relationship a great deal by slightly modifying your own behaviour.

✔ If all else fails, you can always retain your power and walk away.

Useful links

ACAS:

www.acas.org.uk/publications/al05.htm

Bully Online:

www.bullyonline.org/workbully/index.htm

Improve Now.com:

www.improvenow.com

'Super-Sized Stress' at Monster.com:

http://midcareer.monster.com/articles/careerdevelopment/stresseffects

TroubleAtWork:

www.troubleatwork.org.uk/about.asp

Workplace bullying:

www.workplacebullying.co.uk/links.html

Improving leadership skills

There are many myths about leaders—'leaders are born and not made' being a prime example. The truth is that leadership depends on a combination of elements.

The personal qualities of the leader are indeed vital, as are the needs of those being led and the context in which they operate. Although there is no doubt that some personality types thrive better in leadership roles than others, the good news is that leadership skills *can* be learned. In the same way that you can work on your delegation skills and team management techniques, so you can develop the personal qualities you need to be a good leader, like assertiveness and self-confidence. Moreover, leadership is never a finished product; it's an ongoing process that needs continuous nurturing and refinement.

A lack of assertiveness can hold many people back from developing their true potential, particularly in the role of leader. It is one of the keys to successful leadership, together with sensitivity, and a thorough knowledge of the available approaches.

Step one: Understand leadership styles

There are many different styles of leadership. For example, think of three shepherds. The first opens the gate and walks through, allowing the flock to follow—this shepherd *leads from the front*. Another stands behind the sheep and pushes or guides them through, demonstrating a *supportive leadership style*. The third moves from front to back and sometimes to the middle of the flock, demonstrating an *interactive leadership style*.

✔ Learn how to apply different leadership styles as this can help you respond effectively in different situations. For leaders to exist, there must be followers, and the needs of followers change depending on the situation.

Another school of thought recognises four leadership styles: directive, process, creative, and facilitative. Each is related to a personality trait (see diagram below). So, being more

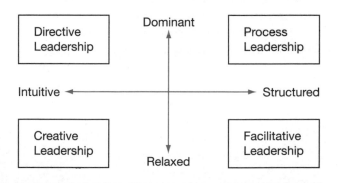

relaxed doesn't mean you can't be a leader. You simply have a natural inclination towards a certain type of leadership.

Evidently, certain styles are suited to particular situations. A structured leader is likely to succeed in a situation where process is important, for example, in running an operation. The relaxed or facilitative leader may be one who manages a professional group of people. Dominant leaders may be needed in organisations where there is a real drive for change. Usually a person with a strongly intuitive style of leadership can cope with most situations short-term.

✔ You may be able to learn other management styles— more dominant, intuitive, or structured—as you become more confident and practised in leadership. Try to work with your preferred style until you are comfortable enough to branch out.

TOP TIP
If your leadership skills have been called into question and the people you supervise seem unmotivated or unproductive, you or your team may be expected to display more commitment. The key to making this change is to think less about what you're doing, and spend more time planning how you do it. Think about how your boss and staff perceive you—and whether their perceptions are accurate. Make sure you seek your boss's advice.

Step two: Learn leadership theory

Business leaders need to understand the guiding principles of their own organisation. Leadership programmes, frequently offered by business schools, provide the foundation of such understanding.

✔ Choose the right course for you. Topics range from business theory to strategic planning to understanding risk. They might also cover organisational behaviour, which analyses what makes people tick (and, therefore, how to manage them), and marketing. You might also find classes on marketplace analysis, encompassing competitor evaluation.

Having well-developed commercial awareness and a good business education will not only give you confidence, but will also help you command respect from others.

TOP TIP
Once you have learned the theory of leadership, you'll need to find an opportunity to put it into practice. You may want to tell your boss that you feel ready for more responsibility. Demonstrate your readiness by proposing to lead a specific project or take on a new area of responsibility, where you can test your skills. It may be helpful to have a mentor to support you at this stage.

Step three: Build self-awareness

Your leadership style is the means by which you communicate with the rest of the organisation. The more self-aware you become, the more effectively it will work for you.

Areas of self-awareness

Self-awareness means understanding and knowing:

- what you are like
- what your preferences are
- what your goals are
- how other people perceive you and your goals
- how you are motivated to achieve them

✔ Try out some of the numerous tests and questionnaires designed to help you explore your personality and preferences. These are widely available from books, the Internet, consultancies, and other sources.

✔ Surveys can also be useful. Most business schools have valuable data on expected leadership behaviours.

✔ Once you've completed this consultation process, combine the information from all these sources to establish a benchmark for yourself.

Step four: Learn from other people's experience

It is often said that 'knowledge is power'. Certainly, a superior level of knowledge will give you an advantage over your peers, making you more suited to leadership positions. Therefore, you should always look for opportunities to learn from others' expertise. Some of the most obvious opportunities you should take advantage of if you can are:

✔ **Coaching.** This is useful in situations where there are behavioural, skills, or confidence gaps.

✔ **Training programmes.** Whether developed within or outside your organisation, training can give you an insight into your abilities as well as expanding them.

✔ **Networking.** Talking to leaders you admire or simply sharing your experiences with others can help you gain a greater awareness of the traits required for leadership.

Step five: Broaden your own experience

In the medium term, there are a number of other strategies you can employ to increase your knowledge, your confidence, and your ability to lead.

✔ **'Stretch' assignments.** These are tasks that extend your horizons but have no negative consequences for your present job should you fail. They are particularly good for people who like to learn on the job.

✔ **Lateral transfers.** You can develop leadership skills more comprehensively by working in different parts of the organisation. This will help you gain a better understanding of how the company works (and why) and provides a useful opportunity for you to work with people outside your 'comfort zone'.

✔ **Benchmarking against peers in other companies.** By gathering information and advice from people who work for different organisations, you can benefit from each other's experience and measure your progress.

✔ **Working outside your comfort zone.** You cannot learn if you always stick within the boundaries of what you know. Take on a project that scares you, challenges you, and offers new experience.

TOP TIP
Many people have trouble transferring leadership skills from outside the workplace into the office environment. Perhaps the outside leadership role is voluntary, or came about because of a passion for that particular project or leisure activity. If so, look at

---

**what allows you to thrive in your external
leadership role. Understanding such factors
as your motivation and the support you
receive may help you to see what is missing
at work. Then you can move towards
creating the right context there too.**

Step six: Apply your leadership skills

Leadership opportunities are often thrust upon us
unexpectedly. However, if you have followed the above
steps and prepared yourself properly, you will be in a
strong position to make the most of the opening. Here
are a few practical tips to help you get off to a good
start.

✔ In most cases, your best bet is to begin with an analysis
of the situation. Decide what is needed, and how you
can best achieve it.

✔ Some leadership positions require you to set the
objectives for others to follow. In these situations,
scheduling, consultation, and team building are essential
to success.

✔ Leaders often need to work as intermediaries between
two groups—those wanting the results (boards or
executive groups, for example), and those who will
deliver the results. In this case you need to establish
good communication channels with both parties.

✔ Try to pick teams that have a good balance between competent managers and energetic, loyal team members. Teams need consistent, positive energy levels to sustain momentum. Therefore, choosing a team according to the mix of talent required, rather than based on friendships or politics, is critical.

✔ If you are trying out new systems or approaches, surround yourself with the right people, create a framework for support, and document the process so you can later evaluate what you have done.

TOP TIP
Leadership capability does not emerge overnight; it takes time and practice. Part of the process involves learning about yourself and your responses to situations that call for leadership. Use this knowledge to assess what has worked and what hasn't, in order to plan your approach next time.

Common mistakes

✗ **You don't realise the changes that a leadership role entails**
People often try to retain the relationships they enjoyed before taking on a leadership position. Leaders, especially those in supervisory roles, must be careful not to let friendships interfere with good judgment.

Be aware, too, that those who know you as a colleague or peer may have a different view of you as a leader.

✗ You mirror other leaders too closely

People new to leadership roles may try to copy a leader they respect, because the person provides an easy model. This can create a false impression of what you are really like, or, worse, make you look foolish for trying to mimic a style incompatible with your own personality. Leadership behaviours come from within. Understand what it is you respect in the other leader and think about how you can best display that attribute. If it doesn't work, don't be afraid to try a new approach.

✗ You don't work at it

Many people hope that they have natural leadership skills, and accept leadership positions without proper training or mental adjustment. This sink-or-swim approach works sometimes, but not always!
Building up leadership skills, increasing awareness of yourself, and developing a positive reputation in the organisation have much more potential for success. It will also give you more room to make mistakes without losing credibility.

✗ You mistake public speaking for leadership

Commanding an audience is a great skill, and many leaders have it. However, it is not the sole requirement. Leaders also need to be problem-solvers and have originality, flair, confidence, self-knowledge, strong interpersonal skills, the ability to listen, vision, good organisational skills, and so on. The ability to 'talk a good fight' is not enough on its own.

STEPS TO SUCCESS

✔ Recognise that leadership is a skill that we can all acquire, rather than a natural talent reserved for a privileged few.

✔ Identify different leadership styles and establish when each one might be appropriate.

✔ Find your own natural style of leadership before developing others.

✔ Learn as much as you can from all the available resources: courses, textbooks, websites, and more experienced colleagues.

✔ Look for opportunities to acquire and practise your leadership abilities. Be brave enough to venture into new territory, expanding your experience, building confidence, and developing new skills.

✔ When presented with a leadership opportunity take time to analyse the situation, set clear objectives, and pick a good team that is competent, loyal, and energetic.

Useful links

Emerald (the trading name of MCB University Press):
www.managementfirst.com/experts/leadership.htm
Entrepreneur.com:
www.entrepreneur.com
The Leadership Trust:
www.leadership.co.uk
University of Exeter, Centre for Leadership Development:
www.ex.ac.uk/leadership

Negotiating the pay rise you deserve

You feel certain that you deserve a pay rise, but you're unsure about how to ask your boss. Many people feel awkward discussing money, but remember that if you don't assert your views, nobody will do it for you. And the chances are that your employer will have no qualms about paying you the bare minimum.

When you make your request, it's very important to think through the issues outlined in this chapter and have as much information to hand as possible. It's also important to know how to respond if you end up receiving a negative answer to the request. Here are some questions that will help you prepare for your negotiations:

- When is the right time to approach your boss for a pay rise?
- How has your performance been, and what documentary evidence can you produce to back up your accomplishments?
- What is the typical salary range for a job such as yours?
- What is the most effective way to make the request?

Step one: Choose your moment

The most obvious time to ask for a pay rise is during your
performance review with your boss. However, it's not
uncommon for supervisors to put off these discussions
for quite a while. It's one of their least favourite things
to do.

✔ If it has been more than a year since your last
performance review and since your last salary increase,
you should approach your supervisor about discussing
your performance and your salary. Be sensitive but
firm: don't make your approach the week before
the company's annual sales conference, but don't
put it off because your supervisor is 'always
too busy'.

✔ Give your boss time to prepare his or her thoughts for
this discussion. Don't put them on the spot by asking for
a meeting in front of other employees, and don't just
drop into his or her office and say, 'I'd like to talk to you
about giving me a pay rise'. If your supervisor is caught
unprepared, they will feel uncomfortable. More
importantly, they may not have the information they need
to give you a definitive answer.

✔ Tell your supervisor that you would like to have a
meeting to discuss your performance, your career
plans, and your salary, and plan for it to last at least
30 minutes.

TOP TIP
All companies go through boom times and
difficult times, and they tend to retrench
and cut costs when things are difficult
financially. But that doesn't mean that
you can't ask for a pay rise. If you have
done a really outstanding job this past year
and can point to concrete contributions,
it is possible that the company might
be able to find some money to reward
your hard work.

Step two: Document your achievements

When you ask for a pay rise, you need to build a business case for why the company should pay you more. You need to show what you have done for them and document why they should reward you.

It is easy to forget all that you have done, but if you keep track of your achievements along the way, you will have an excellent record of what you have contributed.

✔ Keep a job diary or a file of the goals you have achieved and the contribution you have made to the company throughout the year. Be sure to keep track of measurable results from your actions, such as money saved, sales increased, level of quality improved, or percentage of employee retention.

✔ Prepare a one-page executive briefing on your accomplishments to take into your meeting.

TOP TIP

If you go into the salary negotiation meeting with well-prepared documentation of your achievements, you will have a stronger sense of your worth to the company and will feel more self-assured about asking for a pay rise. If you are still nervous, you might consider asking someone to role-play the situation with you so that you can practise beforehand. It is also helpful to visualise the meeting ahead of time and to picture what success would look like. And eliminate any negative talk in your head so that if thoughts come up such as, 'No one ever appreciates what I do,' or 'I never get what I want,' replace these ideas with something positive such as, 'I have worked hard for this company this past year, and I can present a strong case for why I should receive a pay rise.'

Step three: Know your worth in the marketplace

Organisations make a trade-off between paying enough money to keep people motivated and the desire to minimise labour costs. You need to be your own agent and promote your own case. If you don't look out for yourself, the chances are that no one else will.

When companies calculate how much they should pay for a job, they conduct wage surveys to compare salaries within the industry and geographical area. They also conduct internal pay analyses to make sure that comparable jobs within the company receive comparable pay. Such wage and salary information is now available on the Internet (see 'Useful links' on p. 85).

Negotiation is much easier if you know the sort of figure you can reasonably aim for in the current market. Calculating your market value can also be a good confidence booster.

✔ As well as researching your market value externally, try to find out information about the internal pay structure. If you have a human resources department you can ask them for information on what jobs like yours typically pay.

✔ Approach your meeting with your supervisor with a win–win attitude. All successful negotiations end in both parties feeling that they received something of value. Your goal is to get a pay rise. Your supervisor's goal is to have a highly motivated and productive employee.

✔ Remember that pay rises are never given for potential or for what you are 'going to do'. Pay rises are given because of meeting and exceeding performance goals. When you meet with your supervisor, you should be thinking about how your actions and accomplishments have helped to fulfil your supervisor's own goals.

TOP TIP
It is helpful to learn about the salary philosophy of your organisation. For example, does it pay the minimum it can to keep costs down, or does it pay higher than the market rate in order to attract the best employees? Does it tend to give pay rises that are close to the cost of living increase for the year (which is not really a pay rise)? Does it require managers to create a hierarchy among their staff and only give pay rises to the highest performers? If you have an understanding of the company philosophy, you can come to your salary discussion well prepared.

Step four: Discuss, don't dictate

When the meeting begins, remember to build your case—don't rush straight into a request for money. If you have provided evidence to support your claims, it will be much harder for your boss to turn you down.

Equally, be ready to pick up any valuable career tips your boss may offer. This should be a two-way discussion, not a one-way tirade.

✔ Start your negotiation with a description of your accomplishments and contributions, moving into a discussion of how you intend to build on those in the coming year, and what some of your key goals are. Describe your goals in terms of how they will support your boss and make a difference to the company.

✔ Clearly state the amount and percentage of salary increase that you think you deserve and then list your reasons why.

✔ Listen to any objections your boss may have. Consider this discussion as a mentoring session and keep an open mind about what you can learn that will help your progress in the company.

✔ Before trying to overcome any objections, make sure that you communicate your understanding of those objections by paraphrasing what you have heard. This is the first step in negotiation.

✔ Be ready for objections and be prepared to explain why you still deserve a pay rise.

✔ If a salary increase looks unlikely, suggest acceptable alternatives: perhaps you would like some extra holiday time, a change in working conditions, training, or improved benefits. However, if money is your main concern, stay focused on salary as far as possible.

TOP TIP

If you are offered a promotion instead of a pay increase, consider all the factors before you decide whether to accept. First of all, make sure it isn't just a change of job title. If the promotion increases your skills, your responsibilities, and your visibility, and if the company is a start-up or is otherwise strapped for cash, you might agree to take the promotion. But you should also get written agreement from your supervisor that you will have a salary discussion at a predetermined time in the future, such as in three months.

Step five: Accept the decision

There is a possibility that your negotiations will not be successful. This could be for reasons beyond your or your boss's control, so it may not be a reflection on your own performance or abilities.

✔ If you are told that you will not be getting a pay rise at this time, ask what it is you need to do in order to earn an increase. Write down everything you are told.

✔ After the meeting, write a memo thanking your boss for their time, and listing the actions you need to take in order to earn a pay rise.

Common mistakes

✗ You threaten to leave if they don't give you a pay rise

Unless you are really unhappy and were thinking of leaving anyway, this strategy can do you much more harm than good. If you threaten to leave, you are sending the message that you are not that committed to the organisation and are basically out for yourself. This approach is not likely to enhance your career.

✗ You complain to colleagues about your salary

Most organisations prefer that all salary discussions take place only with your immediate supervisor. If you complain about your salary to your colleagues, you are seen as someone who is not a team player, and who is not politically astute. It is very unlikely that you would be promoted or get a pay rise under these circumstances.

✗ You ask fellow employees how much they make

Unless you are in an 'open-book' company, most organisations prefer that salary information be kept private. They are concerned that if employees begin to compare salaries with one another, it may lead some to think that they are being treated unfairly and therefore lead to lower morale. You can get a better idea of your worth by benchmarking similar jobs in your organisation and then doing a search on the Internet for salary ranges for those jobs.

STEPS TO SUCCESS

✔ If you feel that you deserve a pay rise, resolve to do something about it!

✔ Don't rush into the negotiations. Give yourself and your boss time to prepare.

✔ Gather evidence to support your case and get an idea of the kind of figure you should ask for.

✔ Stay calm in the meeting itself. Treat it as a conversation, not a battle.

✔ Have an alternative suggestion if a pay rise is out of the question.

✔ If you don't succeed, learn from the experience. Find out why you didn't get the pay rise this time and what you need to do to succeed next time.

Useful links

Employment360.com:
www.employment360.com/job-search.html
Monster.co.uk:
http://content.monster.co.uk/salaries_benefits
SalarySearch:
www.salarysearch.co.uk

Where to find more help

Agreed: Improve Your Powers of Influence
Terry Gillen
London: Institute of Personnel and Development, 1999
174pp ISBN: 0852928017
The author describes techniques for increasing the influence that
we, as individuals, exert, and for achieving the outcomes that we, as
individuals, desire. He explores each of the key principles involved:
persuading, probing, listening, assertiveness, understanding
behaviours, interpreting body language, giving constructive
criticism, and resolving differences of opinion.

Assertiveness
Terry Gillen
London: Institute of Personnel and Development, 1998
96pp ISBN: 085292769X
The author explores the nature of assertiveness and examines its
effects on our working lives. Focusing on self-assessment and
evaluation, he discusses the process of thinking and behaving
assertively and puts forward a plan to develop more assertiveness in
the reader's own behaviour.

Assertiveness at Work: A Practical Guide to Handling Awkward Situations
Ken Back, Kate Back
New York: McGraw-Hill Education, 1999
224pp ISBN: 0077095332
Aimed at managers, this popular guide offers advice on developing
an assertive approach at work while minimising conflict. It includes
exercises to aid learning and new chapters on negotiating, dealing
with bosses, and assertiveness during times of change.

The Assertiveness Workbook
Randy J. Paterson
Oakland, California: New Harbinger Publications, 2000
200pp ISBN: 1572242094

This book encourages us to express our ideas and stand up for ourselves, both at work and in our personal relationships. Step-by-step guidance uses cognitive-behavioural techniques to improve communication skills, and case studies show how these skills have been used successfully.

Body Language at Work
Adrian Furnham
London: Institute of Personnel and Development, 1999
82pp Management Shapers Series ISBN: 0852927711
This book offers an introduction to the significance of body language and what it reveals about attitudes and emotions. It also presents techniques for interpreting nonverbal gestures and expressions and considers how they might be used in work situations.

Personal Power
Philippa Davies
London: Piatkus Books, 1996
192pp ISBN: 0749916427
Using case histories and role models, the author sets out strategies for developing confidence and charisma, thereby becoming more assertive and successful. Guidance is also given for building up influence and developing the skills of persuasion and negotiation.

When I Say No, I Feel Guilty
Manuel J. Smith
New York: Bantam, 1985
352pp ISBN 0553263900
This best-selling book offers a range of strategies to help people feel comfortable asserting their needs at work and at home. It also offers advice on how to combat manipulation and emotional game-playing by other people.